20 MELODY LINE ARRANGEMENTS +
20 mp3 BACKING TRACKS +
20 mp3 DEMO TRACKS!

PLAYALONG 20/20
VIOLIN
20 EASY POP HITS

To access audio, visit:
www.halleonard.com/mylibrary

Enter Code
6599-6671-9194-3053

ISBN 978-1-78305-986-7

Visit Hal Leonard Online at
www.halleonard.com

Contact us:
Hal Leonard
7777 West Bluemound Road
Milwaukee, WI 53213
Email: info@halleonard.com

In Europe, contact:
Hal Leonard Europe Limited
42 Wigmore Street
Marylebone, London, W1U 2RN
Email: info@halleonardeurope.com

In Australia, contact:
Hal Leonard Australia Pty. Ltd.
4 Lentara Court
Cheltenham, Victoria, 3192 Australia
Email: info@halleonard.com.au

Arrangements by Christopher Hussey.
Backing tracks by Jeremy Birchall & Christopher Hussey.
Violin played by Alexandra Wood.
Audio recorded, mixed and mastered by
Jonas Persson & Imogen Hall.

See first page for the code to access online content

Let It Go (from *Frozen*)

Words & Music by Kirsten Anderson-Lopez and Robert Lopez

Expressively ♩ = 68

22 (Taylor Swift)

Words & Music by Taylor Swift, Max Martin & Johan Schuster

Lightly and excitedly ♩ = 104

All Of Me (John Legend)

Words & Music by John Stephens and Toby Gad

Atlas (from *The Hunger Games: Catching Fire*)

Words & Music by Guy Berryman, Jonathan Buckland, William Champion & Christopher Martin

Best Song Ever (One Direction)

Words & Music by Wayne Hector, John Ryan, Julian Bunetta & Edward Drewett

Jar Of Hearts (Christina Perri)

Words & Music by Christina Perri, Drew Lawrence & Barrett Yeretsian

Just Give Me A Reason (Pink)

Words & Music by Alecia Moore, Jeff Bhasker & Nate Ruess

Last Friday Night (Katy Perry)

Words & Music by Max Martin, Lukasz Gottwald, Bonnie McKee & Katy Perry

Confidently ♩ = 126

Make You Feel My Love (Adele)

Words & Music by Bob Dylan

Tenderly ♩ = 76

Once Upon A Dream (from *Maleficent*)

Words & Music by Sammy Fain & Jack Lawrence

Panic Cord (Gabrielle Aplin)

Words & Music by Jez Ashurst, Gabrielle Aplin & Nicholas Atkinson

Steadily, with a bounce ♩ = 106

Right Place Right Time (Olly Murs)

Words & Music by Stephen Robson, Claude Kelly & Oliver Murs

Smoothly, with expression ♩ = 140

Say Something (A Great Big World, feat. Christina Aguilera)

Words & Music by Mike Campbell, Chad Vaccarino & Ian Axel

A Sky Full Of Stars (Coldplay)

Words & Music by Guy Berryman, Jonathan Buckland, William Champion, Christopher Martin & Tim Bergling

Stay (Rihanna, feat. Mikky Ekko)

Words & Music by Justin Parker & Mikky Ekko

Titanium (David Guetta)

Words & Music by Sia Furler, David Guetta, Giorgio Tuinfort & Nick van de Wall

(2nd time cresc.)

What Makes You Beautiful (One Direction)

Words & Music by Savan Kotecha, Carl Falk & Rami Yacoub

to Coda

D.S. al Coda

Coda

Wrecking Ball (Miley Cyrus)

Words & Music by Stephan Moccio, Sacha Skarbek, Lukasz Gottwald, Henry Russell Walter & Maureen McDonald

Someone Like You (Adele)

Words & Music by Daniel Wilson & Adele Adkins

Smoothly, with tenderness ♩ = 68

Skyfall (from *Skyfall*)

Words & Music by Adele Adkins & Paul Epworth

Powerfully ♩ = 75